JOURNAL TRUMPS HATE

MILLIONS* OF HILARIOUS ACTIVITIES TO HELP GET YOU THROUGH TRUMP'S PRESIDENCY

*ONE HUNDRED THIRTEEN OR SO

JOURNAL TRUMPS HATE

Printed by: Createspace.com

Mr. Trump's quotations are his actual quotations.

Facts about Mr. Trump are supposedly true, except for when they are obviously not.

10 9 8 7 6 5 4 3 2 1

Published 2017 by Kingfisher Books
Kingfisher Press
www.kingfisherpressbooks.com

January, 2017
New York, New York, USA

This book is dedicated to Hugs.

INTRODUCTION

"The human race has one really effective weapon, and that is laughter."
—Mark Twain, immortal satirist

When it comes to people, we're optimists. We believe human beings are innately good. People don't always know what's best for them—just ask the 80s, when parachute pants were an acceptable pantaloon. But philosopher Thomas Hobbes was way off when he called the human race nasty, brutish and short. For starters, if we were short, then where did Yao Ming come from? Outer space? That dude's YUGE.

But secondly, and more seriously, we truly believe in the goodness of humans. Sure, we have the capacity for nasty and brutish acts—war, terrorism, Donald Trump's hair. But at our core, humans have an incredible capacity for love, generosity and peace.

In the early hours of November 9th, 2016, the news of Donald Trump's victory took our faith in humanity and gave a good, vigorous shaking. How the hell could so many Americans vote for Donald Trump, a man who seems to ooze misogyny and bigotry from his pores. Along with many Americans, we went through a wild spectrum of emotions—rage, disbelief, depression. How was the country going to get through this?

In our lifetime, the United States of America has never been this divided. Half (well, let's be honest, 46.1%) of America seems downright jubilant in their certainty that Trump will be an excellent president, one who will help them achieve their dreams. And to all the Trump supporters in America, we believe that you are good people who deserve happiness, safety and prosperity. We sincerely hope Trump makes life better for you.

For the other half (well, let's be honest, 53.9%) of Americans who are a bit more ~~dubious~~ FREAKED THE F**K OUT about Trump's presidency, we're with you. Trump campaigned on a venomous platform of intolerance and bigotry—he essentially campaigned on hate. For those of us who value silly little things like tolerance, inclusion and freedom, we hope Trump listens to us. We hope he surprises us and succeeds in making America great again. Heck—we hope Donald Trump becomes the most tremendous president in the history of the United States of America. Just the best. Just phenomenal.

We hope Donald Trump makes the world a better place—for everybody.

On the off chance that that doesn't happen, here's what we propose: Let's fight hate with love, let's defeat intolerance with acceptance, and let's make a whole lot of fun of Donald Trump. We know that humor won't magically fix all the problems in the world. While it may make Donald Trump's hair more tolerable, humor will not reverse global warming, and it certainly won't eradicate the world of war and terrorism. But it's a damn fine remedy for grief. So dig into this book and remember the words of immortal satirist Tom Robbins:

"All things are possible, laughter is holier than piety, freedom is sweeter than fame, and in the end it's love and love alone that really matters."

With love,
Sam Kaplan & Katie Tonkovich

Use Art Supplies to Find the Perfect

"DONALD TRUMP ORANGE"

WARNING: THIS ACTIVITY MIGHT
COMRPOMISE THE INTEGRITY OF THE
INTRO. PROCEED WITH CAUTION.

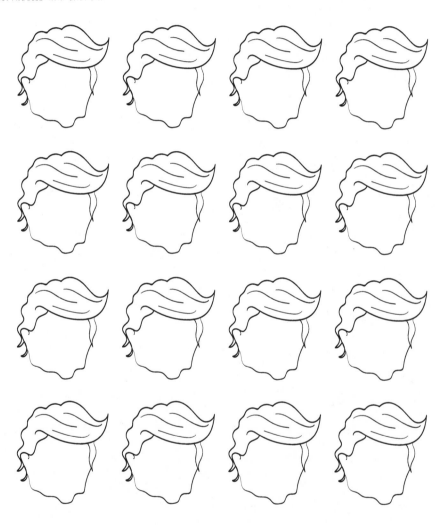

LOVE TRUMPS HATE PLAN #01

FOR ALL OF TODAY, BE AS LOVING AS A GOLDEN RETRIEVER.

DID YOU KNOW?

Donald Trump once got a lump of coal for Christmas and turned it into a diamond.

As a young boy, Donald Trump was given a small loan of $100,000 to start a lemonade stand.

The lemonade stand was a tremendous success, generating nearly $400 in sales.

 DONALD TRUMP WAS ONCE QUIET FOR FIVE WHOLE MINUTES.

START HERE

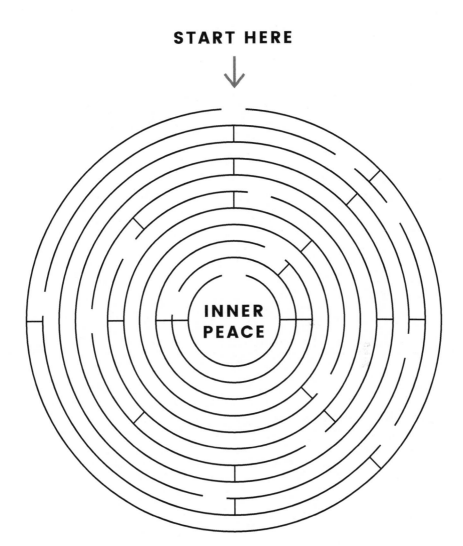

INNER
PEACE

USING FACTS BUT NO FEELINGS

Write a strongly worded essay about Trump:

_____

_____

_____

_____

_____

_____

_____

_____

_____

USING FEELINGS BUT NO FACTS

Write a strongly worded essay about Trump:

COMPLETE THE TRUMP-LIKE CREATURE*

*HELPFUL HINT: IT DOESN'T HAVE TO BE HUMAN

COMPLETE THE TRUMP-LIKE CREATURE:

THREE TRUMPS & A LIE

According to Trump's favorite news source, the internet,
Trump actually said three (or sometimes four) of these things.
Can you figure out which ones he didn't say?

TRUMP ON POLITICS:

A. I'm not a politician, thank goodness.

B. While in politics it is often smart to send out false messages.

C. How stupid are the people of the country to believe this crap?

D. I am not a politician--that's why I will be a phenomenal politician, just phenomenal.

TRUMP ON CONFIDENCE:

A. Everything I've done virtually has been a tremedous success.

B. Big league. That's how I would describe Trump Tower, and, you know, other things.

C. I know how to do it. I really know how to do it.

D. My whole life is about winning. I don't lose often. I almost never lose.

TRUMP ON HIS HAIR AND HANDS:

A. I have better hair than he does, right?

B. I actually don't have a bad hairline.

C. My fingers are long and beautiful, as, it has been well documented, are various other parts of my body.

D. My hands are strong and sturdy, really strong. My hands are absolutely tremendous.

ANSWERS: 1:D, 2:B, 3:D

DID YOU KNOW?

DONALD TRUMP HAS NEVER WON A GAME OF CHESS BECAUSE HE REFUSES TO USE THE QUEEN.

Donald Trump has told the truth at least several times.

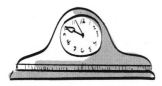

In Donald Trump's home, broken clocks are only right once a day.

ESPECIALLY SPECIAL
ESCAPE SCHEME
★ ★ ★ 01 ★ ★ ★

DECLARE YOUR HOUSE A SOVEREIGN NATION-STATE.

NAME YOUR NEW NATION:

_____

YOUR NATION'S NAME

THEN, CREATE A MOTTO:

Here are some examples:

West Virginia
Montani semper liberi
"Mountain men are always free"

Maryland
Fatti maschii, parole femine
"Manly deeds, womanly words"

Virginia
Sic semper tyrannis
"thus always to tyrants"

Belize
Sub Umbra Floreo
"Under the Shade I Flourish"

Empire of Japan (1868-1947)
"Hoping for establishing international righteousness, preventing communism, creating new culture and actualizing economic connection in East Asia"

Now try a few yourself:

1. _____

2. _____

3. _____

4. _____

Circle your favorite one.

Design Your Nation's Flag:

this could be your headpiece ⎯

or this ⎯

DECLARE YOURSELF ⎯⎯⎯⎯⎯⎯

CHOOSE AN ADJECTIVE LIKE:

SUPREME

BENEVOLENT

ALMIGHTY

JUST

NASTY

HOLY

EL

GLUTEN-FREE

ALTRUISTIC

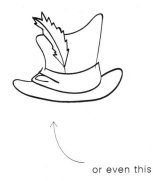

or even this

or this one you draw right here

_____ **OF** _____.

CHOOSE A TITLE LIKE:
RULER
PRESIDENT
QUEEN
DICTATOR
LEADER
CZAR
WOMAN
HEFE
PRIESTESS

YOUR NATION'S NAME

Write your nation's ten laws...

01:

02:

03:

04:

05:

...and make them super nice and inclusive.

06:

07:

08:

09:

10:

Write down your National Anthem:

Choose and draw
YOUR NATION'S ANIMAL*

choose and draw
YOUR NATION'S BIRD*

*HELPFUL HINT: IT COULD BE REAL OR IMAGINARY

choose and draw

YOUR NATION'S
SECRETARY OF _____
(PICK ANYTHING)

DO THIS
RIGHT QUICK
PLAN **005**

REVERSE

GLOBAL

WARMING

MAD-MAN LIB

Without peeking at the next page, fill in the blanks on
this page. Then flip to the other side and copy over
your answers to complete the story.

_____
BODY PART

_____   _____
ADVERB   NEGATIVE ADJECTIVE

_____   _____
COLOR   EMOTION

_____
PLURAL NOUN

_____   _____
ADJECTIVE   PLURAL NOUN

_____
REPEAT SAME BODY PART

_____
VERB ENDING IN ~ED

_____   _____   _____
ADVERB   VERB ENDING IN ~ED   ITEM RICH KIDS OWN

_____   _____
ADVERB   VERB ENDING IN ~ED

_____
ITEM RICH KIDS OWN

_____
REPEAT SAME BODY PART

_____
VERB ENDING IN ~ED

_____   _____   _____
POSITIVE ADJECTIVE   VERB ENDING IN ~ED   COLOR

_____
POSITIVE ADJECTIVE

MAD-MAN LIB

Copy over your answers from the
previous page to complete the story.

As a teenager, Donald Trump was extremely
ashamed of his _____ because it was
                    BODY PART
_____ _____. When his classmates
  ADVERB   NEGATIVE ADJECTIVE
teased him for this, his face would grow
_____ with _____. He yelled at them,
  COLOR   EMOTION
"Stop it, you_____. You are all just a
            PLURAL NOUN
bunch of _____ _____."
         ADJECTIVE   PLURAL NOUN
Later that night, he tried to fix his _____.
                          SAME BODY PART
He tried everything he could think of. He _____
                             VERB ENDING IN −ED
it. He _____ _____ his _____.
     ADVERB   VERB ENDING IN −ED   ITEM RICH KIDS OWN
And he even _____ _____ his
              ADVERB   VERB ENDING IN −ED
_____. When he woke up the next morning,
 ITEM RICH KIDS OWN
he looked at his _____. It still sucked, but
           SAME BODY PART
he didn't cry. Instead, he just _____ his
                     VERB ENDING IN −ED
_____ hair, _____ his _____
  POSITIVE ADJECTIVE   VERB ENDING IN −ED   COLOR
teeth, and went back to school, because that's
how _____ he is.
    POSITIVE ADJECTIVE

ACTIVISM
FOR BEGINNERS
07

RIP OUT THIS TARGET & THROW AN EGG AT HATE.

HATE

[AND THEN CLEAN IT UP]

THREE TRUMPS & A LIE

According to Trump's favorite news source, the internet,
Trump actually said three (or sometimes four) of these things.
Can you figure out which ones he didn't say?

TRUMP ON HUMILITY

A.   I will absolutely apologize sometime hopefully in the distant future
     if I'm ever wrong.

B.   They want to see somebody that's super-competent, and that's me.

C.   I think I am, actually humble. I think I'm much more humble than
     you would understand.

D.   Subtlety and modesty are appropriate for nuns and therapists.

E.   One of the greatest things about me is that I'm so humble.
     I am just phenomenally modest.

TRUMP ON MONEY

F.   My father gave me a small loan of a million dollars.

G.   He's got no money, zero . . . he's got nothing. I mean, he's got nothing.

H.   Part of the beauty of me is that I am very rich.

I.   The point is that you can't be too greedy.

J.   I could throw my name on Chinese pollution and turn
     it into a million dollar enterprise.

TRUMP ON INTELLIGENCE

K.   I'm so smart and brilliant. I'm all the different things.

L.   I'm, like, a really smart person.

M.   I'm like the smart person.

N.   They don't write good.

ANSWERS: 1:E, 2:E, 3:A

SUPER DUPER GENTLE
ANGER OUTLET

009

STOMP
ON THE
FLOOR

(But safely, in sturdy shoes)

LOVE TRUMPS HATE PLAN #10

BRIGHTEN FIVE PEOPLE'S DAY BY SENDING THEM HEARTFELT TEXTS

**FIGHT VIOLENCE
ACTION PLAN
011**

PUNCH a gun

TRUMP QUIZ #1
Select the correct answer

1 Trump's Nickname is:

A. Cheeto Man

B. The Donald

C. Jerk

D. The Trumpster

E. Nick

2 The "J" in Donald J Trump stands for:

A. Jackson

B. Jabroni

C. Jerk

D. Jeronimo

E. John

3 Trump has a board game. It's called:

A. Monopoly

B. Trump: The Game

C. Jerk

D. You're Fired!

E. Corruption

4 Trump and Ringo Starr once appeared on this television show:

A. My So Called Life

B. Friends

C. Jerk

D. Sabrina, the Teenage Witch

E. House of Cards

5 Trump is really afraid of

A. Germs

B. Tax Returns

C. Women

D. Clowns

6 In 1990, Spy Magazine once pranked Donald Trump by:

A. Conning him into signing up for a free trial of "toupee hair gel"

B. Tricking him into investing in "Pear Inc.", a fictitious Apple competitor

C. Duping him into cashing a check for 13 cents

D. Getting him to publicly admit that he supported the non-existent "War on Metaphors."

ANSWERS: 1:B, 2:E, 3:B, 4:D, 5:A, 6:D

Support the grassroots arts by completing this poem:

ROSES ARE RED,
VIOLETS ARE _____
TRUMP IS _____
AND _____

Nice. How about another one?

ROSES ARE RED,
AMERICA'S _____
_____
_____

SUPER DUPER GENTLE
ANGER OUTLET

015

A FIVE-STEP PLAN
TO COMBAT RACISM

STEP 1

Meet somebody of
a different ethnicity.

STEP 2

Talk to that person,
and occasionally flirt respectfully.

STEP 3

Fall in love with that person.

STEP 4

Marry that person.

STEP 5

Have hella babies.

TRUMP QUIZ #2
Select the correct answer

1 Trump once tried to sue an author for calling him a(n):

A. Womanizing douche-bag

B. Millionaire (instead of billionaire)

C. Jerk

D. Unlawful patriarch

E. Human

2 In 1968, Trump avoided the draft because he:

A. Wore women's underwear to the medical exam

B. Fled to Canada

C. Was a jerk

D. Had bad feet

E. Was a conscientious objector

3 The following Trump product actually exists:

A. Trump Ken: A Barbie Doll

B. Success by Trump: a cologne

C. Steak Jerky

D. Cheaties: A crunchy orange chip

E. The Shredderator: A high-end document shredder

4 Trump owned or partially owned the following organization/entity:

A. The Washington Redskins

B. Miss USA

C. Tabasco Hot Sauce

D. MSNB

5 Trump thinks that he could have "nailed" the following woman:

A. Princess Diana

B. Ivanka Trump

C. Jerk

D. Rosie O'Donnell

E. Jessica Rabbit

6 Trump does not believe in:

A. Exercise

B. Handshakes

C. Global Warming

D. "The Movement Against Asbestos"

E. Medicare

F. All of the Above

DID YOU KNOW?

IT ONLY TAKES ONE DONALD TRUMP TO SCREW IN A LIGHT-BULB,

because he intelligently outsources the labor.

The Earth once got confused
and revolved around The Donald,
for three straight days.

DONALD TRUMP REINVENTED THE WHEEL. IT'S CALLED A

JET PLANE.

COMPLETE THE TRUMP-LIKE CREATURE*

*HELPFUL HINT: IT DOESN'T HAVE TO BE HUMAN

LOVE TRUMPS HATE PLAN #22

SAY SOMETHING SUPER SWEET TO YOUR MOTHER. TODAY.

26 WAYS TO NUMB

1 Cryogenically freeze yourself.

2 Find a tall tree in the forest, sit very comfortably, inhale deeply, and then meditate . . . . until 2021.

3 Get SOOOO good at sleeping.

4 Build a dope ass time machine.

these blanks are for you to make some up.

5 _____

_____

6 _____

_____

7 _____

_____

8 _____

_____

YOURSELF UNTIL 2021

9

Draw a wall of booze.

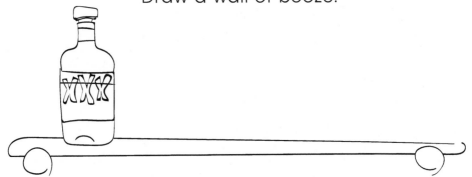

Drink it.

26 WAYS TO NUMB

10 Learn how to lower your heart rate so that your metabolism slows down so much that you're basically asleep.

11 Heroin.*

12 Ice bath.

13 Netflix and chill, like FOREVER.

these blanks are for you to make some up.

14 _____

_____

15 _____

_____

16 _____

_____

17 _____

_____

* please don't do heroin

YOURSELF UNTIL 2021

18

Draw the tallest biggest greasiest heaviest
most-toppingsist burger ever.

Eat it. Food coma.

26 WAYS TO NUMB YOURSELF UNTIL 2021

19 Splice your DNA with a bear and hibernate.

20 Write in this journal. For four years.

21 Stare at a watch.

22 Novocaine yourself.

these blanks are
for you to make
some up.

23 _____

_____

24 _____

_____

25 _____

_____

26 _____

_____

SAVE THE PLANET

ACTION PLAN #42

HUG A TREE HELLA HARD

SUPER REALISTIC
EXTREMELY
SIMPLE PLAN

043

HACK

RUSSIA

THREE TRUMPS & A LIE

According to Trump's favorite news source, the internet,
Trump actually said three (or sometimes four) of these things.
Can you figure out which ones he didn't say?

TRUMP ON LOGIC

A. I've led every debate, number one in every debate, which you know,
and I couldn't say it unless I did.

B. I felt that I was in the military in the true sense because I dealt
with the people.

C. "I think there are two Donald Trumps" and later; "I don't think there
are two Donald Trumps. I think there is one Donald Trump."

D. It rained the other day, in Los Angeles--and you're trying to tell me
Global Warming isn't just a huge hoax?

TRUMP ON RACISM

A. I don't have a racist bone in my body.

B. Well, you know, when it comes to racism and racists, I am the least
racist person there is.

C. Happy Cinco de Mayo! The best taco bowls are made in
Trump Tower Grill. I love Hispanics!

D. I love the Japanese. I don't love sushi. I don't get it. I don't get sushi.

TRUMP ON MORALITY

A. My moral authority is better than his moral authority, that I can
tell you.

B. I love the poorly educated.

C. I have the best ethics.

D. I've said that if Ivanka weren't my daughter, perhaps I would
be dating her.

FILL IN THE _____

WHEN YOUR MIND CAN'T THINK
OF THE ANSWER

1. Living in America over the next four years will be _____

   _____

2. But, it will also be _____

3. I am a little freaked out that _____

   _____

4. But I am confident that _____

   _____

5. I will continue fighting for _____

   _____

6. I will also fight for _____

7. Things may be hard, but I can always depend on _____

   _____

8. One reason I'm optimistic is that _____

9. Another reason I'm hopeful is _____

   _____ .

10. The one thing that always makes me smile is _____

    _____

11. One thing I can do is always _____

12. I can also _____

13. I will never stand for _____

14. Or _____

DID YOU KNOW?

DONALD TRUMP ONCE TRIED TO ERADICATE POVERTY BY GIVING IT A HIGH FIVE.

Young Donald lost a spelling bee because
he spelled the word "apologize" like this:

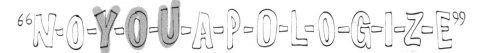

"N-O-Y-O-U-A-P-O-L-O-G-I-Z-E"

Donald Trump once floated into outer
space after shouting "WRONG" to gravity.

CAUSE FOR CONCERN
Trump will be president for:

4	years
28	dog years
47.96	months
52.14	moons
104.28	fortnights
208.57	intolerable weeks
1460	dog garn days
35,040	hours
2,102,400	minutes
126,144,000	seconds
126,144,000,000	milliseconds
126,144,000,000,000	microseconds
126144000000000000	nanoseconds

CAUSE FOR OPTIMISM

Trump will only be president for:

3.99	tropical years
3.99	Gregorian years
3.99	Julian years
0.4	decades
.04	centuries
0.004	millenia
0.00000000001	twinkie years
-4	yesteryears

draw another time
keeping device

Draw elephants and donkeys
living together in peace and harmony.

HERE ARE SOME
HAIKUS ABOUT TRUMP

ONE HAIKU

Summer in 'Merica

Hope swells like beams of
sunshine—

Autumn falls darkly

ANOTHER HAIKU

Face of bright orange

Slimy sausage-finger hands

No high fives for you

NOW WRITE YOUR OWN:

_____

_____

_____

AWESOME JOB! TRY AGAIN:

_____

_____

_____

TELL SOMEONE

MAD-MAN LIB

Without peeking at the next page, fill in the blanks on
this page. Then flip to the other side and copy over
your answers to complete the story.

_____   _____
ADJECTIVE   PLURAL NOUN

_____
VERB ENDING IN -ED

_____
ADJECTIVE

_____
ADJECTIVE

_____
POSITIVE NOUN

_____
POSITIVE ADJECTIVE

_____ ,
ACTIVITY

_____
CELEBRITY

_____   _____
ADVERB   NEGATIVE ADJECTIVE

_____
NOUN

_____
FEELING

_____
FEELING

_____ ,
NOUN

_____
NOUN

_____   _____ .
ADJECTIVE   PLURAL NOUN

_____
NOUN THAT FLIES

_____
RIDICULOUS LOCATION

_____
ADVERB

_____
ADJECTIVE

MAD-MAN LIB

Copy over your answers from the
previous page to complete the story.

Donald Trump woke up on one morning and
devoured a whole bunch of _____ _____
ADJECTIVE   PLURAL NOUN
for breakfast. After that, he _____ his very
VERB ENDING IN -ED
_____ hair. Catching his reflection in the
ADJECTIVE
mirror, he exclaimed, "boy, am I one _____
ADJECTIVE
_____ . I am just so tremendously _____ ."
POSITIVE NOUN   POSITIVE ADJECTIVE

Later that morning, after his daily _____ ,
ACTIVITY
Donald looked at Twitter. _____ had tweeted
CELEBRITY
something _____ _____ about Trump's
ADVERB   NEGATIVE ADJECTIVE
_____ . Trump was extremely _____
NOUN   FEELING
and _____ . He hastily packed his _____ ,
FEELING   NOUN
_____ , and many _____ _____ .
NOUN   ADJECTIVE   PLURAL NOUN
He jumped on his _____ , and traveled to
NOUN THAT FLIES
_____ . After landing, he swore he would
RIDICULOUS LOCATION
never again return to The United States of America.
The people of America were obviously _____
ADVERB
_____ !
ADJECTIVE

WHAT WOULD YOU SAY TO D ONALD TRUMP IF YOU MET HIM?

HEY DONALD,

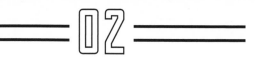

ESPECIALLY SPECIAL
ESCAPE SCHEME
02

CHOOSE ANY PLANET TO COLONIZE.
(Color one in or draw your own somewhere and name it)

Your planet's name: _____

DRAW YOURSELF A SUPER AWESOME ROCKET SHIP OR FLYING ANIMAL

ESPECIALLY SPECIAL
ESCAPE SCHEME
02

WHO DO YOU INVITE AND WHY?

HUMAN 1:
REASON / SKILLS:

HUMAN 2:
REASON / SKILLS:

HUMAN 3:
REASON / SKILLS:

HUMAN 4:
REASON / SKILLS:

HUMAN 5:
REASON / SKILLS:

HUMAN 6:
REASON / SKILLS:

HUMAN 7:
REASON / SKILLS:

HUMAN 8:
REASON / SKILLS:

HUMAN 9:
REASON / SKILLS:

HUMAN 10:
REASON / SKILLS:

CHART YOUR PATH THROUGH SPACE.

SUPER
NOVA

EROS

SPACE CADETS

START

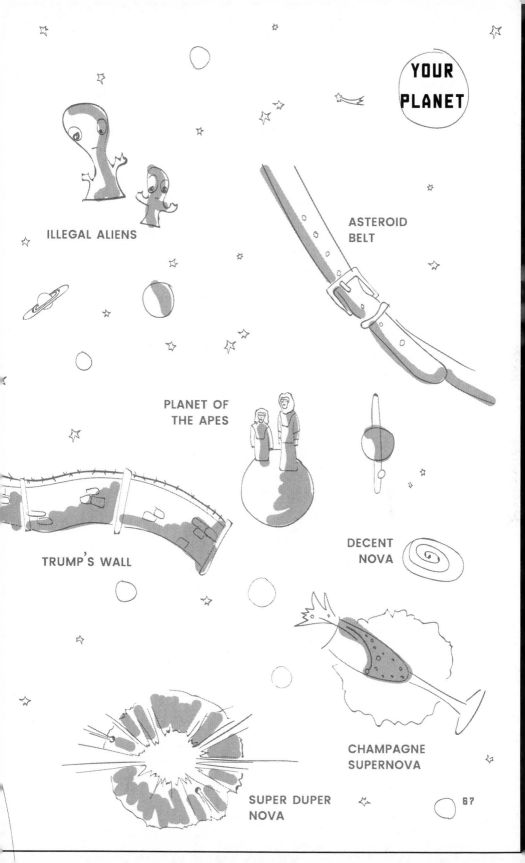

DRAW YOUR SETTLEMENT

ASSIGN YOUR INVITEES GOVERNMENTAL ROLES*

Hear ye, hear ye, by proclamation of _____
YOUR NAME

_____ shall be the _____
HUMAN ONE   GOVERNMENT ROLE

_____ shall be the _____
HUMAN ONE   GOVERNMENT ROLE

_____ shall be the _____
HUMAN ONE   GOVERNMENT ROLE

_____ shall be the _____
HUMAN ONE   GOVERNMENT ROLE

_____ shall be the _____
HUMAN ONE   GOVERNMENT ROLE

_____ shall be the _____
HUMAN ONE   GOVERNMENT ROLE

_____ shall be the _____
HUMAN ONE   GOVERNMENT ROLE

_____ shall be the _____
HUMAN ONE   GOVERNMENT ROLE

_____ shall be the _____
HUMAN ONE   GOVERNMENT ROLE

and _____ shall be the _____
HUMAN ONE   GOVERNMENT ROLE

Let it be known across the land, that these fine humans shall perform their governmental duities to the utmost of their awesome skills.

Hip hip _____ !
WORD OF YOU CHOICE

*HELPFUL HINT: MAKE SURE THEY ARE SEVERELY UNDER-QUALIFIED
AND/OR DO NOT BELIEVE IN THE DUTIES OF THEIR ROLE.

WRITE AND NEGOTIATE A SUPER NICE TREATY WITH PLANET EARTH'S UNITED STATES OF AMERICA.

Dear Donald Trump's USA,

The people of our planet and the people of Earth's United States of America hereby agree to the following:

1 All current and future disputes shall be resolved by

_____
CHOOSE GENTLE ACTION

2 Planet Earth shall freely share all of its _____ ,
RESOURCE
_____ , and _____ .
RESOURCE   RESOURCE

3 In exchange, our planet shall freely share all of its _____ ,
RESOURCE
_____ , and _____ .
RESOURCE   RESOURCE

4 In perpetuity, Donald J Trump shall never again _____

_____

_____

_____ or _____ .

With Love,

_____   _____
YOU   DATE

Congratulations,
you have now achieved

EVERLASTING

INTERGALACTIC

PEACE

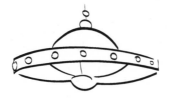

DID YOU KNOW?

Donald Trump once attempted to eliminate world hunger by eating it for breakfast.

DONALD TRUMP DEFINITIVELY PROVED THAT THE CHICKEN CAME FIRST JUST BY TWEETING THAT THE EGG WAS TOTAL BS.

Donald Trump fought and won thirty-four wars just by being a man of the people.

FIGHT VIOLENC
ACTION PLAN
064

LIGHTLY

PUNCH

A PRIVILEGED
WHITE MALE*

*but then hug him

SUPER DUPER GENTLE
ANGER OUTLET

065

CRUMPLE THIS PAGE,

AND THEN RECYCLE IT.

HAVE YOU CHECKED YOUR WHITE PRIVILEGE ENOUGH?

A HANDY FLOWCHART

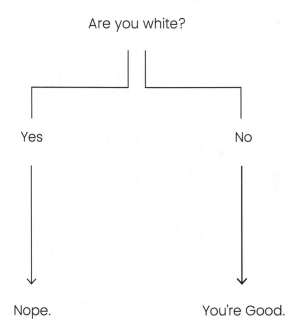

Are you white?

Yes

No

Nope.

You're Good.

ACTION PLAN #67

SUCKER PUNCH GLOBAL WARMING

COMPLETE THE TRUMP-LIKE CREATURE:

FILL IN THE _____

1. Donald Trump eats _____ for breakfast.

2. Donald Trump's hair is reminiscent of a _____.

3. The five ingredients that make Donald Trump are _____
    _____.

4. Donald Trump's ties are so long because _____
    _____.

5. Trump's favorite hashtag is _____.

6. Donald Trump basically invented _____.

7. When young Donald was five, he really sucked at _____
    _____.

8. In addition to germs, Donald is really afraid of _____.

9. If The Donald were a food, he would be _____.

10. If The Donald were a rapper, his MC name would be
    _____.

11. If The Donald were an animal, he would be a _____.

12. Donald Trump never learned how to _____.

13. If Donald Trump were born poor, he would have grown up to be
    a _____.

14. Donald Trump worships _____.

15. The only thing Donald Trump has ever lost is _____
    _____.

DID YOU KNOW?

Donald Trump CAN fit a square peg into a round hole.

DONALD TRUMP ONCE FILED FOR MORAL BANKRUPTCY. TWICE.

The Donald's tears are so awesome they can power hydroelectric damns. We are still reliant on fossil fuels because the Donald never cries.

DRAW DONALD TRUMP'S FACE IN CHEETOS.

WRITE 'DONALD J. TRUMP' IN EXTREMELY CRAPPY HANDWRITING.

LOVE TRUMPS HATE PLAN #68

GIVE A COOKIE TO A STRANGER*

DRAW YOUR COOKIE

unless they are gluten-free

*in which case you should bake
them a gluten-free cookie*

*which won't really be a cookie

DID YOU KNOW?

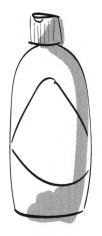

SHAMPOO ONCE SAW DONALD'S HAIR AND HAD TO SEE A THERAPIST FOR 12 YEARS.

Donald Trump was cast in A Few Good Men, but his role was eventually given to Jack Nicholson because the truth couldn't handle Donald Trump.

Donald Trump once stopped a tsunami just by interrupting it.

WRITE DOWN 10 THINGS YOU
USED TO LOVE DOING AS A KID.

1

2

3

4

5

6

7

8

9

10

NOW DO THEM!

WRITE DOWN YOUR 10 LEAST
FAVORITE THINGS DONALD TRUMP DOES.

1

2

3

4

5

6

7

8

9

10

NOW NEVER DO THEM!

LOVE TRUMPS HATE PLAN #81

REMEBER YOU
ARE AWESOME

FIGHT VIOLENCE
ACTION PLAN
082

KARATE

CHOP

A

BRO.

(LOVINGLY)

**FUN PRANKS
TO PLAY
ON DONALD
#83**

STEP 1
Draw a small Trump here.

STEP 2
Rip this page out.

STEP 3
Turn it into an origami boat
(google it).

STEP 4
Check the tides.

STEP 5
Float the boat to Mexico.

STEP 6
Now Trump's in Mexico
and he doesn't like that!
Hah.

**FUN PRANKS
TO PLAY
ON DONALD
#83**

...CONTINUED

Draw Trump trying to climb over his wall to get back into the USA.

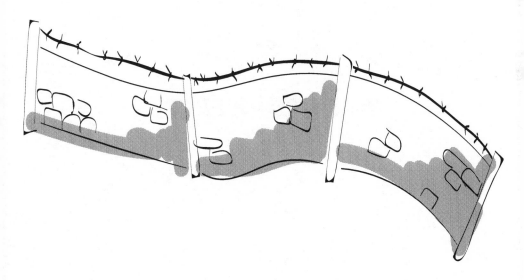

ESPECIALLY SPECIAL
ESCAPE SCHEME
03

ZOMBIE DEATH PLAN.

ESCAPE SCHEME 03

STEP ONE:

Create a cure for Zombieism.

Circle the proper ingredients:

MSG

cephalopod

a garden burger

unrequited love

a single drop of empathy

_____
MAKE ONE YOURSELF

singing the blues

raw steak

ketchup

porcupine needles

kombucha

_____
MAKE ONE YOURSELF

STEP TWO

Hire a mad scientist to create a four-year time-release "Zombie Cure" medicine.

Draw the mad scientist in their lab.
Make sure you color in the ingredients correctly!

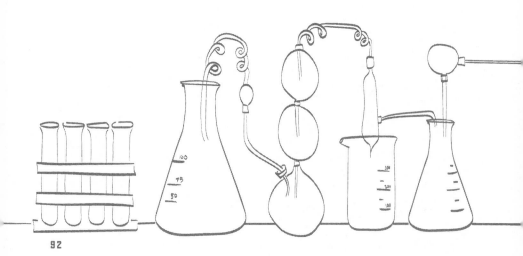

ESCAPE SCHEME
03

STEP THREE
Capture a zombie.

Document your capture plan:

ESCAPE SCHEME 03

STEP FOUR
Fly to a desert island with your new zombie friend.

Draw you and Zombie on the island:

STEP FIVE
Take "Zombie Cure."

STEP SIX
Feed "Zombie Cure" to
your new zombie friend.

STEP SEVEN
Allow your zombie friend to nibble on your
pinkie toe. Now you are both zombie friends!

STEP EIGHT
Zombie around for four years.

STEP NINE
Rehumanize.*

STEP TEN
Fly back to the USA.

STEP ELEVEN
Boom — it is now 2021!

*assuming, of course, that you chose the correct ingredients, and that the mad scientist mixed them in the right ratios, and that the four-year-time-release (while unheard of in the entirety of medical history up until this point) activated on the exact right day for both you and your zombie friend, and that when you rehumanized slightly before your zombie friend (as you took your zombie cure first) you were able to evade said zombie friend for the few minutes before they re-humanized, and that your newly humanized zombie friend didn't just murder you anyways for having the cure to zombieism this whole time but forcing them to continue being a zombie for four years simply because you didn't want to live in the Trumpocracy.

ACTIVISM
FOR BEGINNERS
94

CRY ALL OVER THIS PAGE, THEN DRAW HEARTS WITH YOUR TEARS.

ACTUALLY

MAKE AMERICA
GREAT AGAIN.

COMPLETE THE TRUMP-LIKE CREATURE*

*HELPFUL HINT: IT DOESN'T HAVE TO BE HUMAN

LOVE TRUMPS HATE PLAN #97

BUY A DOZEN FLOWERS AND GIVE THEM ALL AWAY

PUNCH YOUR PENCIL THROUGH ALL THE WORDS THAT HAVE TO DO WITH TRUMP

Trump   Tower   awesome   wall   nepotism

happy   happy   joy   joy   Drumpf   dolphins

hot   sauce   archipelago   nepotism   paste

racist honey sunshine flamboyant sexist pig

bubbles   sparkles   megalomaniac   fireworks

ants   pants   plaid   douchey   douche

chandelier   hot-toddy   crumble   succulent

demoralize   philanthropy   misanthropy

narcissist   evolution   surprise   lotion

jackpot   smelly   farts   barking

spiders inclusive ballet autumnal fancy free

SUPER DUPER GENTLE
ANGER OUTLET

096

BUILD TRUMP TOWER OUT OF LEGOS AND THEN DISASSEMBLE IT

PASTE POLAROIDS OR
DRAW YOUR DESTRUCTION

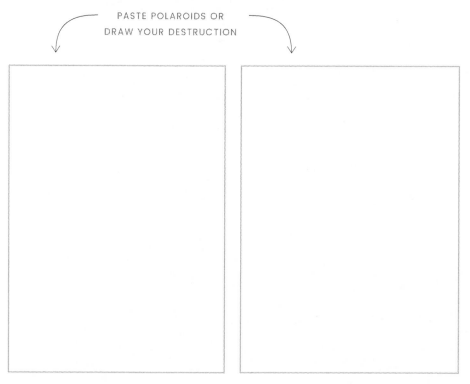

before   after

COMPLETE THE TRUMP-LIKE CREATURE:

NAME YOUR CHILD ANYTHING BUT DONALD

FILL IN THE _____
<small>EMPTY BULLET CARTRIDGES</small>

1. Donald Trump is so ridiculously _____.

2. The most tremendous thing about The Donald is all of his

_____.

3. My most favorite things about Donald are his

_____, his _____, and his

_____.

4. 2013 was stupendously _____.

5. 2018 will be incredibly _____.

6. The Donald is to hair

as _____ is/are to _____.

7. The Donald is to hands

as _____ is/are to _____.

8. Donald Trump's natural smell can best be described as

_____.

9. If Donald Trump had a super power it would obviously be

_____.

10. The only thing The Donald has ever in his life been ever so

slightly wrong about is _____

_____

_____

_____

_____.

<small>HELPFUL HINT: IF YOU'VE RAN OUT OF ROOM, FEEL FREE TO
KEEP GOING IN THE MARGINS AND/OR ON THE PREVIOUS PAGE</small>

THREE TRUMPS & A LIE

According to Trump's favorite news source, the internet,
Trump actually said three (or sometimes four) of these things.
Can you figure out which ones he didn't say?

TRUMP ON WOMEN

A. I will be phenomenal to the women. I want to help women.

B. I will be so good to women. I cherish women. I will be so good to women. I will work hard to protect women.

C. Women love me. If anyone can tell you that, it's me, because it's true.

D. There's nobody that's better to women.

TRUMP'S NUANCED OPINIONS

A. We should be focused on magnificently clean and healthy air and not distracted by the expensive hoax that is global warming!

B. The Bible means a lot to me, but I don't want to get into specifics. . . . I don't want to get into verses.

C. What do I know about it? All I know is what's on the internet.

D. Why do I want to drain the swamp? Because it's a swamp. I mean would you want alligators on your golf course? Of course you wouldn't.

TRUMP ON CHINA

A. Listen, you motherf***ers, we're going to tax you 25 percent.

B. I have visited Tokyo on many occasions. I love the Chinese.

C. The concept of global warming was created by and for the Chinese in order to make U.S. manufacturing non-competitive.

D. Look at what China is doing to our country, they are using our country...as a piggy bank to rebuild China.

ANSWERS: 1:C, 2:D, 3:B

ACTION PLAN #104

SERIOUSLY, JUST PUNCH GLOBAL WARMING IN THE FACE.

SUPER DUPER GENTLE
ANGER OUTLET

105

YELL LOUDL

LOVE TRUMPS HATE PLAN #106

DOODLE A WHOLE BUNCH
OF HEARTS AND FLOWERS.

DON'T BE AFRAID TO
DOODLE ON THIS PAGE, TOO.

A HEART, FOR REFERENCE

STEP ONE:

WRITE "DONALD TRUMP" OVER AND OVER IN PENCIL

STEP TWO

ERASE ALL THIS, VIGOROUSLY

FUN PRANKS
TO PLAY
ON DONALD
109

STEP 1

Draw Donald Trump on this page.

STEP 2

Turn this page into a paper airplane.

STEP 3

Attempt to throw it in the trash from afar.

STEP 4

Don't give up until you make it.

STEP 5

But then actually grab it out of the trash and recycle it.

DID YOU KNOW?

Donald Trump once fell in love seventeen times in a single day.

Unrelatedly, he has seventeen mirrors in his residence.

THE DONALD ONCE KILLED THREE BIRDS WITH ONE STONE.

If you give The Donald six hours to chop down a tree, he will spend the first four sharpening his knife, which he will then use to eat a steak while hired laborers chop down the tree.

FILL IN THE _____

THE STARE OF A CONFUSED PERSON

The biggest difference between Abraham Lincoln and Donald Trump is that The Donald _____ _____.

Donald Trump has a _____ temperament.

The Donald's America has become _____.

In 2032, Donald Trump will be _____.

In secret, when nobody is looking, Donald loves to _____ _____.

Donald Trump's very first word was _____. His next two were _____ and _____.

The opposite of Donald Trump is _____.

Donald's favorite television show is _____.

Trump looks at himself in the mirror every morning and says _____ _____.

Donald Trump is so wealthy that _____ _____.

Donald Trump is so _____ that _____ _____.

SUPER REALISTIC
EXTREMELY
SIMPLE PLAN
112

BE REALLY NICE TO EVERYBODY FOR THE ENTIRETY OF TRUMP'S PRESIDENCY

Before we leave you, here are
50 REAL IDEAS TO HELP YOU GET THROUGH TRUMP'S PRESIDENCY: PART 1

1. Treat yourself to a massage once a month for the duration of Trump's presidency.

2. Let the sun shine on your face every day.

3. Chocolate.

4. Meditate. Start with five minutes.

5. Go on a nice, short walk in the middle of your work day.

6. Work 75% as hard as usual at work for one week.

7. Blast your favorite song and sing along.

8. Go for a walk in nature.

9. Give a stranger a compliment. But not like a creepy one. Be nice. Don't be creepy.

10. Buy yourself a super nice pillow. Or even a bed!

11. Make more time for your friends.

12. Be generous with your laughter. (Laughing is better than not laughing)

13. Take a nice bath.

14. Go to the beach.

15. Take a sweet vacation at least once a year during Trump's presidency.

16. Sing in the shower.

17. Dance!

18. You're not too old to look for shapes in the clouds.

19. Do something new and fun once a month for the duration of Trump's presidency (go ice skating, see to a play, listen to a comedy show, experience the circus).

20. Sit in nature. Listen.

21. Smell jasmine.

22. Remember to have a giggle fit every once in a while.

23. Read an awesome book.

50 REAL IDEAS TO HELP YOU GET
THROUGH TRUMP'S PRESIDENCY: PART 2

24. Watch your favorite comedy from when you were little.

25. Reach out to a friend you haven't talked to in a while.

26. Go take a yoga class.

27. Give longer, better hugs.

28. Breathe.

29. Take a road trip.

30. Be somebody's secret santa every month.

31. Dance to the song that makes you happiest.

32. Spend (at least) ten minutes outside every day.

33. Find yourself a secret spot.

34. Plan an amazing date. For your friend.

35. Go on a weekend getaway.

36. Remember to watch the sunset.

37. Give yourself permission to eat junk food every once in a while.

38. Eat a piece of fruit every day.

39. Enjoy a meal in silence.

40. Plan an amazing date. For yourself.

41. Snuggle with something furry and adorable.

42. Be super thankful for everybody in your life.

43. Avoid screens. Start with five minutes.

44. Surprise a loved one with a small gift.

45. Volunteer.

46. Reconnect with an old friend.

47. Cook something new.

48. Listen to your favorite comedian.

49. Explore a new city in the United States.

50. Adopt a puppy from the shelter.

ACTION PLAN #110

RECYCLE THE PAGES OF THIS BOOK WHEN YOU ARE FINISHED

Want More Books Like This?

KINGFISHERPRESSBOOKS.COM

ABOUT THE AUTHORS

KATIE TONKOVICH

Katie is a visual designer living in Oakland. If she spent half as much time paying attention as she spent sketching and doodling, then perhaps she would have a more robust bio.

SAM KAPLAN

Sam is a writer and therapist living in Oakland, California. The three things he needs for both professions are coffee, a beard and humor.

ONE LAST THING

We truly hope you had fun with this book.
We believe there is no greater cure for the
Trumpocracy than a perfect mix of laughter
and tears (a 17:1 ratio is ideal). Yes, these will
be a tough four years. In fact, some days may
even suck. But we can do it. Keep smiling,
keep fighting for what's right, and also,
here's a baby donkephant.

Made in the USA
San Bernardino, CA
12 January 2017